Weekly Ov

13   Monday

Top To-Dos
Schedule
Today's Notes

14   Tuesday

Top To-Dos
Schedule
Today's Notes

Weekly Overview

15 Wednesday   16 Thursday

Top To-Dos	Top To-Dos
Schedule	Schedule
Today's Notes	Today's Notes

Weekly Overview

17   Friday

Top To-Dos
Schedule
Today's Notes

18   Saturday

Top To-Dos
Schedule
Today's Notes

Weekly Overview

19   Sunday

Top To-Dos

Schedule

Today's Notes

20   Monday

Top To-Dos

Schedule

Today's Notes

Weekly Overview

21 Tuesday

Top To-Dos

Schedule

Today's Notes

22 Wednesday

Top To-Dos

Schedule

Today's Notes

Weekly Overview

23   Thursday   24   Friday

Top To-Dos	Top To-Dos
Schedule	Schedule
Today's Notes	Today's Notes

Weekly Overview

25　Saturday

Top To-Dos
Schedule
Today's Notes

26　Sunday

Top To-Dos
Schedule
Today's Notes

Weekly Overview

27 Monday

Top To-Dos

Schedule

Today's Notes

28 Tuesday

Top To-Dos

Schedule

Today's Notes

Weekly Overview

29   Wednesday   30   Thursday

Top To-Dos	Top To-Dos
Schedule	Schedule
Today's Notes	Today's Notes

Weekly Overview

01 Friday

Top To-Dos

Schedule

Today's Notes

02 Saturday

Top To-Dos

Schedule

Today's Notes

Weekly Overview

03   Sunday   04   Monday

Top To-Dos	Top To-Dos
Schedule	Schedule
Today's Notes	Today's Notes

Weekly Overview

05 Tuesday

Top To-Dos
Schedule
Today's Notes

06 Wednesday

Top To-Dos
Schedule
Today's Notes

Weekly Overview

07 Thursday | 08 Friday

07 Thursday	08 Friday
Top To-Dos	Top To-Dos
Schedule	Schedule
Today's Notes	Today's Notes

Weekly Overview

09   Saturday

Top To-Dos
Schedule
Today's Notes

10   Sunday

Top To-Dos
Schedule
Today's Notes

Weekly Overview

11   Monday

| 12   Tuesday

Top To-Dos

Top To-Dos

Schedule

Schedule

Today's Notes

Today's Notes

Weekly Overview

13   Wednesday   14   Thursday

Top To-Dos	Top To-Dos
Schedule	Schedule
Today's Notes	Today's Notes

Weekly Overview

15   Friday

Top To-Dos
Schedule
Today's Notes

16   Saturday

Top To-Dos
Schedule
Today's Notes

Weekly Overview

17   Sunday

Top To-Dos

Schedule

Today's Notes

18   Monday

Top To-Dos

Schedule

Today's Notes

Weekly Overview

19 Tuesday   20 Wednesday

Top To-Dos	Top To-Dos
Schedule	Schedule
Today's Notes	Today's Notes

Weekly Overview

21 Thursday   22 Friday

Top To-Dos	Top To-Dos
Schedule	Schedule
Today's Notes	Today's Notes

Weekly Overview

23 Saturday

Top To-Dos

Schedule

Today's Notes

24 Sunday

Top To-Dos

Schedule

Today's Notes

Weekly Overview

25 Monday

Top To-Dos
Schedule
Today's Notes

26 Tuesday

Top To-Dos
Schedule
Today's Notes

Weekly Overview

27   Wednesday   28   Thursday

Top To-Dos	Top To-Dos
Schedule	Schedule
Today's Notes	Today's Notes

Weekly Overview

29 Friday

Top To-Dos
Schedule
Today's Notes

30 Saturday

Top To-Dos
Schedule
Today's Notes

Weekly Overview

31 Sunday

Top To-Dos
Schedule
Today's Notes

01 Monday

Top To-Dos
Schedule
Today's Notes

Weekly Overview

02 Tuesday

Top To-Dos
Schedule
Today's Notes

03 Wednesday

Top To-Dos
Schedule
Today's Notes

Weekly Overview

04 Thursday   05 Friday

Top To-Dos	Top To-Dos
Schedule	Schedule
Today's Notes	Today's Notes

Weekly Overview

06 Saturday   07 Sunday

Top To-Dos	Top To-Dos
Schedule	Schedule
Today's Notes	Today's Notes

Weekly Overview

08   Monday

Top To-Dos
Schedule
Today's Notes

09   Tuesday

Top To-Dos
Schedule
Today's Notes

Weekly Overview

10 Wednesday

Top To-Dos

Schedule

Today's Notes

11 Thursday

Top To-Dos

Schedule

Today's Notes

Weekly Overview

12 Friday

Top To-Dos

Schedule

Today's Notes

13 Saturday

Top To-Dos

Schedule

Today's Notes

Weekly Overview

14   Sunday   15   Monday

Top To-Dos	Top To-Dos
Schedule	Schedule
Today's Notes	Today's Notes

Weekly Overview

16   Tuesday

Top To-Dos

Schedule

Today's Notes

17   Wednesday

Top To-Dos

Schedule

Today's Notes

Weekly Overview

18   Thursday

Top To-Dos
Schedule
Today's Notes

19   Friday

Top To-Dos
Schedule
Today's Notes

Weekly Overview

20 Saturday

| 21 Sunday

Top To-Dos	Top To-Dos
Schedule	Schedule
Today's Notes	Today's Notes

Weekly Overview

22 Monday

| 23 Tuesday |

Top To-Dos	Top To-Dos
Schedule	Schedule
Today's Notes	Today's Notes

Weekly Overview

24   Wednesday   25   Thursday

Top To-Dos	Top To-Dos
Schedule	Schedule
Today's Notes	Today's Notes

Weekly Overview

26   Friday

Top To-Dos	
Schedule	
Today's Notes	

27   Saturday

Top To-Dos	
Schedule	
Today's Notes	

Weekly Overview

28   Sunday

Top To-Dos

Schedule

Today's Notes

29   Monday

Top To-Dos

Schedule

Today's Notes

Weekly Overview

30   Tuesday

Top To-Dos

Schedule

Today's Notes

01   Wednesday

Top To-Dos

Schedule

Today's Notes

Weekly Overview

02 Thursday   03 Friday

Top To-Dos	Top To-Dos
Schedule	Schedule
Today's Notes	Today's Notes

Weekly Overview

04 Saturday

Top To-Dos

Schedule

Today's Notes

05 Sunday

Top To-Dos

Schedule

Today's Notes

Weekly Overview

06 Monday

Top To-Dos
Schedule
Today's Notes

07 Tuesday

Top To-Dos
Schedule
Today's Notes

Weekly Overview

08　Wednesday　09　Thursday

Top To-Dos	Top To-Dos
Schedule	Schedule
Today's Notes	Today's Notes

Weekly Overview

10   Friday   11   Saturday

Top To-Dos	Top To-Dos
Schedule	Schedule
Today's Notes	Today's Notes

Weekly Overview

12　Sunday　13　Monday

Top To-Dos	Top To-Dos
Schedule	Schedule
Today's Notes	Today's Notes

Weekly Overview

14   Tuesday

Top To-Dos

Schedule

Today's Notes

15   Wednesday

Top To-Dos

Schedule

Today's Notes

Weekly Overview

16　Thursday　　17　Friday

Top To-Dos	Top To-Dos
Schedule	Schedule
Today's Notes	Today's Notes

Weekly Overview

18   Saturday   19   Sunday

Top To-Dos	Top To-Dos
Schedule	Schedule
Today's Notes	Today's Notes

Weekly Overview

20 Monday

Top To-Dos
Schedule
Today's Notes

21 Tuesday

Top To-Dos
Schedule
Today's Notes

Weekly Overview

22 Wednesday 23 Thursday

Top To-Dos	Top To-Dos
Schedule	Schedule
Today's Notes	Today's Notes

Weekly Overview

24   Friday

Top To-Dos
Schedule
Today's Notes

25   Saturday

Top To-Dos
Schedule
Today's Notes

Weekly Overview

26 Sunday

Top To-Dos

Schedule

Today's Notes

27 Monday

Top To-Dos

Schedule

Today's Notes

Weekly Overview

28   Tuesday   29   Wednesday

Top To-Dos	Top To-Dos
Schedule	Schedule
Today's Notes	Today's Notes

Weekly Overview

30   Thursday   31   Friday

Top To-Dos	Top To-Dos
Schedule	Schedule
Today's Notes	Today's Notes

Weekly Overview

01 Saturday

Top To-Dos
Schedule
Today's Notes

02 Sunday

Top To-Dos
Schedule
Today's Notes

Weekly Overview

03 Monday

| 04 Tuesday |

Top To-Dos	Top To-Dos
Schedule	Schedule
Today's Notes	Today's Notes

Weekly Overview

05 Wednesday 06 Thursday

Top To-Dos	Top To-Dos
Schedule	Schedule
Today's Notes	Today's Notes

Weekly Overview

07 **Friday**	08 **Saturday**
Top To-Dos	Top To-Dos
Schedule	Schedule
Today's Notes	Today's Notes

Weekly Overview

09   Sunday

Top To-Dos
Schedule
Today's Notes

10   Monday

Top To-Dos
Schedule
Today's Notes

Weekly Overview

11 Tuesday

| 12 Wednesday |

Top To-Dos	Top To-Dos
Schedule	Schedule
Today's Notes	Today's Notes

Weekly Overview

13 Thursday

Top To-Dos

Schedule

Today's Notes

14 Friday

Top To-Dos

Schedule

Today's Notes

Weekly Overview

15   Saturday   16   Sunday

Top To-Dos	Top To-Dos
Schedule	Schedule
Today's Notes	Today's Notes

Weekly Overview

17 Monday

Top To-Dos
Schedule
Today's Notes

18 Tuesday

Top To-Dos
Schedule
Today's Notes

Weekly Overview

19 Wednesday   20 Thursday

Top To-Dos	Top To-Dos
Schedule	Schedule
Today's Notes	Today's Notes

Weekly Overview

21   Friday

Top To-Dos
Schedule
Today's Notes

22   Saturday

Top To-Dos
Schedule
Today's Notes

Weekly Overview

23   Sunday

Top To-Dos

Schedule

Today's Notes

24   Monday

Top To-Dos

Schedule

Today's Notes

Weekly Overview

25   Tuesday   26   Wednesday

Top To-Dos	Top To-Dos
Schedule	Schedule
Today's Notes	Today's Notes

Weekly Overview

27 Thursday

Top To-Dos
Schedule
Today's Notes

28 Friday

Top To-Dos
Schedule
Today's Notes

Weekly Overview

29   Saturday   30   Sunday

Top To-Dos	Top To-Dos
Schedule	Schedule
Today's Notes	Today's Notes

Weekly Overview

31   Monday

Top To-Dos
Schedule
Today's Notes

01   Tuesday

Top To-Dos
Schedule
Today's Notes

Weekly Overview

02   Wednesday   03   Thursday

Top To-Dos	Top To-Dos
Schedule	Schedule
Today's Notes	Today's Notes

Weekly Overview

04   Friday   05   Saturday

Top To-Dos	Top To-Dos
Schedule	Schedule
Today's Notes	Today's Notes

Weekly Overview

06 Sunday	**07 Monday**
Top To-Dos	Top To-Dos
Schedule	Schedule
Today's Notes	Today's Notes

Weekly Overview

08   Tuesday   09   Wednesday

Top To-Dos	Top To-Dos
Schedule	Schedule
Today's Notes	Today's Notes

Weekly Overview

10 Thursday

| 11 Friday |

Top To-Dos	Top To-Dos
Schedule	Schedule
Today's Notes	Today's Notes

Weekly Overview

12　Saturday　　13　Sunday

Top To-Dos	Top To-Dos
Schedule	Schedule
Today's Notes	Today's Notes

Weekly Overview

14   Monday

Top To-Dos
Schedule
Today's Notes

15   Tuesday

Top To-Dos
Schedule
Today's Notes

Weekly Overview

16   **Wednesday**   17   **Thursday**

Top To-Dos	Top To-Dos
Schedule	Schedule
Today's Notes	Today's Notes

Weekly Overview

18   Friday

Top To-Dos
Schedule
Today's Notes

19   Saturday

Top To-Dos
Schedule
Today's Notes

Weekly Overview

20 Sunday

Top To-Dos

Schedule

Today's Notes

21 Monday

Top To-Dos

Schedule

Today's Notes

Weekly Overview

22   Tuesday   23   Wednesday

Top To-Dos	Top To-Dos
Schedule	Schedule
Today's Notes	Today's Notes

Weekly Overview

24   Thursday   25   Friday

Top To-Dos	Top To-Dos
Schedule	Schedule
Today's Notes	Today's Notes

Weekly Overview

26   Saturday   27   Sunday

Top To-Dos	Top To-Dos
Schedule	Schedule
Today's Notes	Today's Notes

Weekly Overview

28   Monday   01   Tuesday

Top To-Dos	Top To-Dos
Schedule	Schedule
Today's Notes	Today's Notes

Weekly Overview

02   **Wednesday**   03   **Thursday**

Top To-Dos	Top To-Dos
Schedule	Schedule
Today's Notes	Today's Notes

Weekly Overview

04　Friday

Top To-Dos
Schedule
Today's Notes

05　Saturday

Top To-Dos
Schedule
Today's Notes

Weekly Overview

06   Sunday   07   Monday

Top To-Dos	Top To-Dos
Schedule	Schedule
Today's Notes	Today's Notes

Weekly Overview

08   Tuesday   09   Wednesday

Top To-Dos	Top To-Dos
Schedule	Schedule
Today's Notes	Today's Notes

Weekly Overview

10   Thursday

Top To-Dos

Schedule

Today's Notes

11   Friday

Top To-Dos

Schedule

Today's Notes

Weekly Overview

12   Saturday   13   Sunday

Top To-Dos	Top To-Dos
Schedule	Schedule
Today's Notes	Today's Notes

Weekly Overview

14 Monday

Top To-Dos
Schedule
Today's Notes

15 Tuesday

Top To-Dos
Schedule
Today's Notes

Weekly Overview

16   Wednesday   17   Thursday

Top To-Dos	Top To-Dos
Schedule	Schedule
Today's Notes	Today's Notes

Weekly Overview

18 Friday

	19 Saturday
Top To-Dos	Top To-Dos
Schedule	Schedule
Today's Notes	Today's Notes

Weekly Overview

20   Sunday   21   Monday

Top To-Dos	Top To-Dos
Schedule	Schedule
Today's Notes	Today's Notes

Weekly Overview

22   Tuesday   23   Wednesday

Top To-Dos	Top To-Dos
Schedule	Schedule
Today's Notes	Today's Notes

Weekly Overview

24 Thursday   25 Friday

Top To-Dos	Top To-Dos
Schedule	Schedule
Today's Notes	Today's Notes

Weekly Overview

26   Saturday   27   Sunday

Top To-Dos	Top To-Dos
Schedule	Schedule
Today's Notes	Today's Notes

Weekly Overview

28 Monday

Top To-Dos
Schedule
Today's Notes

29 Tuesday

Top To-Dos
Schedule
Today's Notes

Weekly Overview

30   Wednesday   31   Thursday

Top To-Dos	Top To-Dos
Schedule	Schedule
Today's Notes	Today's Notes

Weekly Overview

01 Friday	02 Saturday
Top To-Dos	Top To-Dos
Schedule	Schedule
Today's Notes	Today's Notes

Weekly Overview

03   Sunday   04   Monday

Top To-Dos	Top To-Dos
Schedule	Schedule
Today's Notes	Today's Notes

Weekly Overview

05 Tuesday

Top To-Dos

Schedule

Today's Notes

06 Wednesday

Top To-Dos

Schedule

Today's Notes

Weekly Overview

07   Thursday   08   Friday

Top To-Dos	Top To-Dos
Schedule	Schedule
Today's Notes	Today's Notes

Weekly Overview

09   Saturday   10   Sunday

Top To-Dos	Top To-Dos
Schedule	Schedule
Today's Notes	Today's Notes

Weekly Overview

11 Monday

Top To-Dos
Schedule
Today's Notes

12 Tuesday

Top To-Dos
Schedule
Today's Notes

Weekly Overview

13 Wednesday 14 Thursday

Top To-Dos	Top To-Dos
Schedule	Schedule
Today's Notes	Today's Notes

Weekly Overview

15   Friday

Top To-Dos
Schedule
Today's Notes

16   Saturday

Top To-Dos
Schedule
Today's Notes

Weekly Overview

17   Sunday

18   Monday

Top To-Dos	Top To-Dos
Schedule	**Schedule**
Today's Notes	Today's Notes

Weekly Overview

19   Tuesday

Top To-Dos

Schedule

Today's Notes

20   Wednesday

Top To-Dos

Schedule

Today's Notes

Weekly Overview

21 Thursday

Top To-Dos
Schedule
Today's Notes

22 Friday

Top To-Dos
Schedule
Today's Notes

Weekly Overview

23   Saturday

24   Sunday

Top To-Dos	Top To-Dos
Schedule	Schedule
Today's Notes	Today's Notes

Weekly Overview

25   Monday   26   Tuesday

Top To-Dos	Top To-Dos
Schedule	Schedule
Today's Notes	Today's Notes

Weekly Overview

27 Wednesday 28 Thursday

Top To-Dos	Top To-Dos
Schedule	Schedule
Today's Notes	Today's Notes

Weekly Overview

29 Friday

Top To-Dos

Schedule

Today's Notes

30 Saturday

Top To-Dos

Schedule

Today's Notes

Weekly Overview

01 Sunday	02 Monday
Top To-Dos	Top To-Dos
Schedule	Schedule
Today's Notes	Today's Notes

Weekly Overview

03   Tuesday

Top To-Dos

Schedule

Today's Notes

04   Wednesday

Top To-Dos

Schedule

Today's Notes

Weekly Overview

05   Thursday   06   Friday

Top To-Dos	Top To-Dos
Schedule	Schedule
Today's Notes	Today's Notes

Weekly Overview

07 Saturday   08 Sunday

Top To-Dos	Top To-Dos
Schedule	Schedule
Today's Notes	Today's Notes

Weekly Overview

09   Monday   10   Tuesday

Top To-Dos	Top To-Dos
Schedule	Schedule
Today's Notes	Today's Notes

Weekly Overview

11 Wednesday 12 Thursday

Top To-Dos	Top To-Dos
Schedule	Schedule
Today's Notes	Today's Notes

Weekly Overview

13   Friday   14   Saturday

Top To-Dos	Top To-Dos
Schedule	Schedule
Today's Notes	Today's Notes

Weekly Overview

15　Sunday

Top To-Dos

Schedule

Today's Notes

16　Monday

Top To-Dos

Schedule

Today's Notes

Weekly Overview

17   Tuesday   18   Wednesday

Top To-Dos	Top To-Dos
Schedule	Schedule
Today's Notes	Today's Notes

Weekly Overview

19   **Thursday**   20   **Friday**

Top To-Dos	Top To-Dos
Schedule	Schedule
Today's Notes	Today's Notes

Weekly Overview

21 Saturday

Top To-Dos

Schedule

Today's Notes

22 Sunday

Top To-Dos

Schedule

Today's Notes

Weekly Overview

23 Monday

Top To-Dos

Schedule

Today's Notes

24 Tuesday

Top To-Dos

Schedule

Today's Notes

Weekly Overview

25   Wednesday   26   Thursday

Top To-Dos	Top To-Dos
Schedule	Schedule
Today's Notes	Today's Notes

Weekly Overview

27   Friday

Top To-Dos

Schedule

Today's Notes

28   Saturday

Top To-Dos

Schedule

Today's Notes

Weekly Overview

29 Sunday

Top To-Dos

Schedule

Today's Notes

30 Monday

Top To-Dos

Schedule

Today's Notes

Weekly Overview

31   Tuesday   01   Wednesday

Top To-Dos	Top To-Dos
Schedule	Schedule
Today's Notes	Today's Notes

Weekly Overview

02 Thursday

| 03 Friday |

Top To-Dos	Top To-Dos
Schedule	Schedule
Today's Notes	Today's Notes

Weekly Overview

04 Saturday 05 Sunday

Top To-Dos	Top To-Dos
Schedule	Schedule
Today's Notes	Today's Notes

Weekly Overview

06 Monday | 07 Tuesday

Top To-Dos	Top To-Dos
Schedule	Schedule
Today's Notes	Today's Notes

Weekly Overview

08   Wednesday   09   Thursday

Top To-Dos	Top To-Dos
Schedule	Schedule
Today's Notes	Today's Notes

Weekly Overview

10   Friday

Top To-Dos

Schedule

Today's Notes

11   Saturday

Top To-Dos

Schedule

Today's Notes

Weekly Overview

12 Sunday   13 Monday

Top To-Dos	Top To-Dos
Schedule	Schedule
Today's Notes	Today's Notes

Weekly Overview

14   Tuesday

Top To-Dos

Schedule

Today's Notes

15   Wednesday

Top To-Dos

Schedule

Today's Notes

Weekly Overview

16 Thursday

| 17 Friday |

Top To-Dos	Top To-Dos
Schedule	Schedule
Today's Notes	Today's Notes

Weekly Overview

18   Saturday   19   Sunday

Top To-Dos	Top To-Dos
Schedule	Schedule
Today's Notes	Today's Notes

Weekly Overview

20 Monday	21 Tuesday
Top To-Dos	Top To-Dos
Schedule	Schedule
Today's Notes	Today's Notes

Weekly Overview

22　Wednesday　23　Thursday

Top To-Dos	Top To-Dos
Schedule	Schedule
Today's Notes	Today's Notes

Weekly Overview

24   Friday

Top To-Dos
Schedule
Today's Notes

25   Saturday

Top To-Dos
Schedule
Today's Notes

Weekly Overview

26   Sunday

Top To-Dos
Schedule
Today's Notes

27   Monday

Top To-Dos
Schedule
Today's Notes

Weekly Overview

28 Tuesday

Top To-Dos
Schedule
Today's Notes

29 Wednesday

Top To-Dos
Schedule
Today's Notes

Weekly Overview

30   Thursday   01   Friday

Top To-Dos	Top To-Dos
Schedule	Schedule
Today's Notes	Today's Notes

Weekly Overview

02 Saturday

Top To-Dos
Schedule
Today's Notes

03 Sunday

Top To-Dos
Schedule
Today's Notes

TMA's Due

TMA	Due Date	✔	Grade

iCMA's Due

iCMA	Due Date	✔	Grade

Exam/EMA Planning

➞ ....

➞ ....

➞ ....

➞ ....

➞ ....

Other Notes/Due Dates

....

....

....

TMA
Planning

➡️ ....

➡️ ....

➡️ ....

➡️ ....

➡️ ....

Other Notes/Due Dates

....

....

....

TMA Planning

 ....

 ....

 ....

 ....

 ....

Other Notes/Due Dates

....

....

....

TMA Planning

Other Notes/Due Dates

TMA
Planning

 ....

 ....

 ....

 ....

 ....

Other Notes/Due Dates

....

....

....

TMA
Planning

 ....

 ....

 ....

 ....

 ....

Other Notes/Due Dates

....

....

....

TMA
Planning

 ....

 ....

 ....

 ....

 ....

Other Notes/Due Dates

....

....

....

TMA
Planning

Other Notes/Due Dates

TMA
Planning

 ....

 ....

 ....

 ....

 ....

Other Notes/Due Dates

....

....

....

TMA
Planning

Other Notes/Due Dates

TMA
Planning

Other Notes/Due Dates

TMA
Planning

 ....

 ....

 ....

 ....

 ....

Other Notes/Due Dates

....

....

....

TMA
Planning

 ....

 ....

 ....

 ....

 ....

Other Notes/Due Dates

....

....

....

TMA
Planning

Other Notes/Due Dates

TMA
Planning

 ....

 ....

 ....

 ....

 ....

Other Notes/Due Dates

....

....

....

Exam/EMA Planning

→ ....

→ ....

→ ....

→ ....

→ ....

Other Notes/Due Dates

....

....

....

Exam/EMA Planning

⟶ ....

⟶ ....

⟶ ....

⟶ ....

⟶ ....

Other Notes/Due Dates

....

....

....

Important Notes for Assignments

TMA: _____

_____
_____
_____
_____
_____
_____
_____
_____
_____
_____
_____
_____
_____
_____
_____
_____
_____
_____
_____
_____
_____
_____
_____

Important Notes for Assignments

TMA: _____

_____

_____

_____

_____

_____

_____

_____

_____

_____

_____

_____

_____

_____

_____

_____

_____

_____

_____

_____

_____

_____

_____

_____

_____

Important Notes for Assignments

TMA: _____

_____

_____

_____

_____

_____

_____

_____

_____

_____

_____

_____

_____

_____

_____

_____

_____

_____

_____

_____

_____

_____

_____

Important Notes for Assignments

TMA: _____

_____

_____

_____

_____

_____

_____

_____

_____

_____

_____

_____

_____

_____

_____

_____

_____

_____

_____

_____

Important Notes for Assignments

TMA: _____

_____

_____

_____

_____

_____

_____

_____

_____

_____

_____

_____

_____

_____

_____

_____

_____

_____

_____

_____

_____

Important Notes for Assignments

TMA: _____

_____
_____
_____
_____
_____
_____
_____
_____
_____
_____
_____
_____
_____
_____
_____
_____
_____
_____
_____
_____
_____
_____
_____

Important Notes for Assignments

TMA: _____

_____
_____
_____
_____
_____
_____
_____
_____
_____
_____
_____
_____
_____
_____
_____
_____
_____
_____
_____
_____
_____
_____
_____
_____
_____

Important Notes for Assignments

TMA: _____

_____

_____
_____
_____
_____
_____
_____
_____
_____
_____
_____
_____
_____
_____
_____
_____
_____
_____
_____
_____
_____
_____
_____
_____

Important Notes for Assignments

TMA: _____

_____

_____

_____

_____

_____

_____

_____

_____

_____

_____

_____

_____

_____

_____

_____

_____

_____

_____

_____

_____

_____

_____

_____

_____

_____

_____

Important Notes for Assignments

TMA: _____

_____

_____
_____

_____
_____

_____
_____

_____
_____

_____
_____

_____
_____

_____
_____

_____
_____

_____
_____

_____
_____

_____

Important Notes for Assignments

TMA: _____

Important Notes for Assignments

TMA: _____

_____
_____
_____
_____
_____
_____
_____
_____
_____
_____
_____
_____
_____
_____
_____
_____
_____
_____
_____
_____
_____
_____
_____

Important Notes for Assignments

TMA: _____

Important Notes for Assignments

TMA: _____

_____
_____
_____
_____
_____
_____
_____
_____
_____
_____
_____
_____
_____
_____
_____
_____
_____
_____
_____
_____
_____

Important Notes for Assignments

TMA: _____

Important Notes for Assignments

TMA: _____

_____

_____

_____

_____

_____

_____

_____

_____

_____

_____

_____

_____

_____

_____

_____

_____

_____

_____

_____

_____

Important Notes for Assignments

TMA: _____

Important Notes for Assignments

TMA: _____

Important Notes for Assignments

TMA: _____

_____

_____

_____

_____

_____

_____

_____

_____

_____

_____

_____

_____

_____

_____

_____

_____

_____

_____

_____

_____

_____

_____

Monthly Action Planner

SEPTEMBER

OCTOBER

NOVEMBER

DECEMBER

JANUARY

FEBRUARY

Monthly Action Planner

MARCH

APRIL

MAY

JUNE

JULY

Yearly Goals

list your academic goals:

_____

_____

_____

_____

_____

_____

_____

PLAN YOUR BEST YEAR

Yearly Goals

list your academic goals:

_____

_____

_____

_____

_____

_____

_____

PLAN YOUR BEST YEAR

Other Notes

Other Notes

Other Notes

Other Notes

Other Notes

Other Notes

Other Notes

Other Notes

Other Notes

Other Notes

Other Notes

Made in the USA
Las Vegas, NV
18 September 2021